THE SOUTHWEST DIVISION

BY JOHN WALTERS AND ROBERT E. SCHNAKENBERG

THE DALLAS MAVERICKS · THE HOUSTON ROCKETS · THE MEMPHIS GRIZZLIES · THE NEW ORLEANS HORNETS · THE SAN ANTONIO SPURS

Published in the United States of America by
The Child's World® • PO Box 326
Chanhassen, MN 55317-0326

800-599-READ • www.childsworld.com

ACKNOWLEDGEMENTS

The Child's World®: Mary Berendes,
Publishing Director

Editorial Directions, Inc.: E. Russell Primm, Editorial
Director and Line Editor; Katie Marsico, Managing
Editor; Caroline Wood, Editorial Assistant; Susan
Hindman, Copy Editor; John Barrett, Proofreader;
Tim Griffin, Indexer; Kevin Cunningham, Fact
Checker; James Buckley Jr. and Jim Gigliotti,
Photo Researchers and Photo Selectors

Manuscript consulting and photo research by
Shoreline Publishing Group LLC.

The Design Lab: Kathleen Petelinsek,
Design and Page Production

Photos:
Bettmann/Corbis: 36
Paul Buck/AFP/Getty: 38
Nathaniel S. Butler/NBAE/Getty: 41
Tim DeFrisco/NBAE/Getty: 30
Stephen Dunn/Getty: 9
Focus on Sport/Getty: 16, 45
Jesse D. Garrabrant/NBAE/Getty: 15
Eric Gay/AP: 1, 37
Bill Haber/AP: 32
Glenn James/NBAE/Getty: 13
Tim Johnson/AP: 18
Bill Kostroun/AP: 23
Ronald Martinez/Getty: 4
Donna McWilliam/AP: 20
Fernando Medina/NBAE/Getty: 34
Joe Murphy/NBAE/Getty: 5, 26
David J. Phillip/AP: Cover
Mike Powell/Getty: 8
Matt Sayles/AP: 12
Ron Schwane/AP: 10
Sports Gallery: 29
Kim Stallnecht/AP: 22
Rick Stewart/Getty: 7
Chuck Stoody/AP: 24
Mark J. Terrill/AP: 33
Ted S. Warren/AP: 40
Matt York/AP: 2

LIBRARY OF CONGRESS
CATALOGING-IN-PUBLICATION DATA

Walters, John (John Andrew)
 The Southwest Division / by John Walters and
Robert E. Schnakenberg.
   p. cm. — (Above the rim)
 Includes index.
  ISBN 1-59296-559-8 (library bound : alk. paper)
 1. National Basketball Association—History—Juvenile
literature. 2. Basketball—Southwest, New—History—
Juvenile literature. I. Schnakenberg, Robert. II. Title.
III. Series.
  GV885.515.N37W36   2006
  796.323'64'0973—dc22
  2005026209

TABLE OF CONTENTS

INTRODUCTION

The Southwest Division of the National Basketball Association (NBA) may have been new in 2004–05, but it didn't take long to get up and running. In fact, some of the best basketball in the league was played in the Southwest that season.

First, a little background. Four of the five teams in the Southwest Division—the Dallas Mavericks, Houston Rockets,

The Spurs celebrated after winning their third NBA title in 2004–05.

The Hornets and Grizzlies are the two youngest franchises in the Southwest Division.

Memphis Grizzlies, and San Antonio Spurs—have played together since the mid-1990s, originally in the NBA's Midwest Division, which had seven teams in its final season in 2003–04. (The Mavericks, Rockets, and Spurs go back even further, to 1980—long before the Grizzlies came into existence.)

In 2004, when the NBA expanded to 30 teams, it grouped its clubs into six divisions for the first time. The Midwest officially was **disbanded,** and the Mavericks, Rockets, Grizzlies, and Spurs were joined by the New Orleans Hornets—which had been playing in the Central Division—in the new Southwest Division.

While the division may not have a lot of history behind it, its teams certainly do. Southwest franchises can boast of NBA MVP winners such as Moses Malone (1982) and Hakeem Olajuwon (1994) of the Houston Rockets, and David Robinson (1995) and Tim Duncan (2002 and 2003) of the San Antonio Spurs. The Rockets were NBA champions in 1994 and 1995, and the Spurs have won it all three times since 1999.

There are several natural rivalries that add to the flavor of the Southwest, too. All three of the NBA's Texas teams are in the division, so they vie for bragging rights in the Lone Star State. And, of course, the holdovers from the Midwest Division are familiar foes. Even the Hornets played a season in the Midwest in 1989 (while based in Charlotte) before moving to the Central Division.

Oh, and then there's the quality of the basketball. San Antonio won 59 games to take the Southwest in the division's first season in 2004–05, while Dallas added 58 victories and Houston had 51. That made the Southwest the only division in the NBA that year to include three teams with 50 or more wins.

The biggest win of all, of course, belonged to the Spurs. That victory came over the Detroit Pistons in Game 7 of the **NBA Finals,** and it lifted San Antonio to the league title for 2004–05.

Team	Year Founded	Home Arena	Year Arena Opened	Team Colors
Dallas Mavericks	1980	American Airlines Center	2001	Blue, white, and silver
Houston Rockets	1967	Toyota Center	2003	Red and white
Memphis Grizzlies	1995	FedExForum	2004	Blue and black
New Orleans Hornets	1988	New Orleans Arena	1999	Teal, purple, and white
San Antonio Spurs	1967	SBC Center	2002	Metallic silver, black, teal, fuchsia, and orange

CHAPTER ONE

THE DALLAS MAVERICKS

Mark Aguirre helped the Mavericks make the playoffs for the first time in 1983–84.

The "Mavs" are the youngest of the three NBA franchises that make their home in Texas, and they are the only ones who haven't won an NBA championship—yet.

The franchise debuted in the 1980–81 season. Coach Dick Motta, who only two years earlier had guided the Washington Bullets to an NBA title, tried everything to get this new team to win games. Once, during halftime of a game, he entered the locker room with a live tiger

to scare the laziness out of his players. Another time, he ordered his center, Wayne Cooper, to **goaltend** a free throw attempt.

Nothing worked. The Mavs finished a league-worst 15–67 in their rookie season. After that, their win totals climbed annually, from 15 to 28 to 38 to 43 to 44. During the 1983–84 season, forward Mark Aguirre finished second in the NBA in scoring (29.5 points per game) and became the first Maverick All-Star. That season was also the first Dallas made the playoffs.

In 1986–87, the Mavs rolled to a 55–27 record and won the Midwest Division. Aguirre and guard

Rolando Blackman is the Mavericks' all-time leading scorer.

Seven-footer Roy Tarpley was a towering forward.

Rolando Blackman, both All-Stars who had arrived in Dallas as rookies in the franchise's second season, were the featured players. **Power forward** Sam Perkins was a rising star. Off the bench, the Mavs had two more forwards—7-foot Roy Tarpley and 6-foot-10 Detlef

Forward Michael Finley led the league in minutes played in both 1998 (3,394) and 2000 (3,464).

Guard Steve Nash helped the Mavericks reach new heights.

Schrempf—who later in their careers would each win NBA **Sixth Man** of the Year awards.

Dallas beat Seattle 151–129 in the first postseason game that season and then lost three straight. Motta quit and was replaced by John McLeod, who led Dallas to a 53-win season in 1987–88. After losing in the playoffs again, the Mavericks went into a tailspin for a decade. Six different coaches took their turn on the sideline. In 1992–93, Dallas won just 11 games, and it began the next season with a 1–23 record before finishing 13–69. Big "D" stood for "disaster."

In the early 1990s, Dallas used three consecutive top-10 **draft** picks to select guard Jimmy Jackson (1992), forward Jamal Mashburn (1993), and guard Jason Kidd (1994). Hailed as the "Three Js," this trio was supposed to return the Mavericks to glory. Alas, the Three Js began to stand for Jealousy, Juvenile, and Jinxed. Jackson, Mashburn, and Kidd feuded off the court and had trouble sharing the ball on it. The Mavericks eventually traded all three of them. Dallas also traded Tony Dumas and Loren Meyer. They got Michael Finley, Sam Cassell, and A. C. Green.

In 1998, forward Dirk Nowitzki, just 20 years old and 7 feet tall, arrived from Germany. Nowitzki plays a nearly flawless game and has a deadly outside shot that, because of his height, is virtually unblockable. By the 2002–03 season, Nowitzki had established himself as a star, ranking in the league's top 10 in both scoring and rebounding.

Finley, Steve Nash (a Canadian with a rock-star persona), and Nowitzki formed the trio that Dallas

On February 23, 2002, against the Sacramento Kings, Dirk Nowitzki set an NBA record for the most defensive rebounds in a game (21) without an offensive rebound.

Forward Dirk Nowitzki goes all out at both ends of the floor.

The Mavericks closed the 2004–05 season with 16 wins in 18 games after former NBA star Avery Johnson took over as head coach.

had hoped the Three Js would be. With a potent, pass-happy offense, Dallas became one of the league's most entertaining teams—and one of the best, too. Under the tutelage of coach Don Nelson, the Mavericks won 53 regular-season games in 2000–01, 57 games in 2001–02, and a franchise-record 60 games in 2002–03. That year,

Nowitzki averaged 25.1 points per game for the league's highest-scoring club.

In the 2002–03 postseason, Dallas won each seven-game series over both the Portland Trail Blazers and the Sacramento Kings. But the Mavericks' championship hopes ended in the conference finals, when eventual NBA champion San Antonio won in six games.

Dallas has not returned to such heights since. Nash has moved on to Phoenix, and Avery Johnson has succeeded Nelson as coach. But Nowitzki remains a powerful force, and newcomers such as point guard Jason Terry and center Erick Dampier helped Dallas forge a 58–24 record in 2004–05. The Mavericks finished just one game behind the Spurs in the race for the first Southwest Division title.

Jason Terry runs the Mavericks' offense from the point-guard position.

CHAPTER TWO

THE HOUSTON ROCKETS

For 27 seasons, the Houston Rockets had the reputation of being a solid franchise but one that couldn't quite make it into championship orbit. Then in the mid-1990s, while Chicago's Michael Jordan was off playing baseball, the Rockets won a pair of NBA titles.

The franchise began in 1967 as the San Diego Rockets. Their first draft pick that season was Pat Riley, who would go on to greater success as a coach than as a player. San Diego finished the season with the NBA's worst record, 15–67.

Rewarded with the top overall pick in the 1968 draft, San Diego chose Elvin Hayes. As a rookie, "the Big E" led the NBA in scoring (28.4 points per game) and was fourth in rebounding. Hayes, a 6-foot-10 power forward, finished in the top three in the league in both scoring and rebounding the next two seasons. Before his fourth season, 1971–72, the Rockets moved to Houston, where the Big E had attended college. The Rockets did not have a permanent home arena, however, so they often played home games in smaller southwestern cities. Hayes averaged a team-best 25.2 points per game that year.

Calvin Murphy sank 206 of 215 free throws in 1980–81 to set the single-season free throw percentage record, .958. Thirteen seasons later, Murphy was sitting in the front row when Mahmoud Abdul-Rauf of the Denver Nuggets stepped to the line on the final day of the season with the chance to break Murphy's record. Abdul-Rauf had hit 219 of 228, with one last free throw remaining. He missed, finishing the season 219 of 229 for a .956 percentage.

Rudy Tomjanovich, once a popular player in Houston, became a popular coach for the Rockets.

Two of his teammates would become the most popular players in franchise history. Rudy Tomjanovich, a sweet-shooting 6-foot-8 forward, would later coach Houston to its championships. Calvin Murphy, a 5-foot-9 dynamo, would retire as the franchise's all-time leading scorer. Both spent their entire careers in Rockets' uniforms.

In 1972, the NBA moved the franchise from the Western Conference to the Central Division in the Eastern Conference. There it remained for eight seasons, until 1980–81, when the league relocated it to the Midwest Division.

The move agreed with the Rockets, who, despite a 40–42 record, advanced all the way to the NBA Finals. Though the Rockets boasted

**Ralph Sampson (No. 50) and Hakeem Olajuwon (No. 34) gave
the Rockets a pair of skyscrapers in the frontcourt.**

6-foot-10 center Moses Malone (who would end his career with three MVP trophies), the Boston Celtics ended the Rockets' unlikely championship run in six games.

In both 1983 and 1984, the Rockets had the number-one over-all picks in the NBA draft. They chose 7-foot-4 Ralph Sampson and 6-foot-10 Hakeem Olajuwon, respectively. The "Twin Towers," as the pair became known, returned the Rockets to the NBA Finals in 1986. Again, Houston stunned a defending champion L.A. Lakers team. To win Game 5, Sampson made a famous off-balance **buzzer-beater.** Houston, however, once again fell to the Celtics in the finals.

Over the next decade, Olajuwon, a Nigerian native who had played soccer—not basketball—as a youth, became the league's dominant center. He was graceful and, thanks to his soccer back-ground, blessed with extraordinary footwork in the **low post.**

In 1993–94, Olajuwon, known by now as

Rudy Tomjanovich was the victim of the most violent on-court act in NBA history. In December 1977, a fight broke out between Kermit Washington of the Los Angeles Lakers and Kevin Kunnert of the Houston Rockets. Tomjanovich ran over to the fracas, where-upon Washington, a karate expert, wheeled around and punched him in the face. Tomjanovich suffered massive facial injuries and missed the rest of the season.

Hall of Famer Clyde Drexler had his uniform number retired in 2000.

A Rocket has led the NBA in rebounding six different seasons. Elvin Hayes was the first, Hakeem Olajuwon did it twice, and Moses Malone did it three times. Malone had the highest single-season average, 17.6, in 1978–79.

"the Dream," earned the the league's Most Valuable Player award after leading the Rockets to a 58-24 record. In the NBA Finals, the Rockets faced the New York Knicks, who had the league's next-best center of the era, Patrick Ewing. Olajuwon averaged 26.9 points, 9.1 rebounds, and 3.9 blocked shots against Ewing. The Rockets won the series, four games to three, at last bringing a championship to Houston.

In 1995, Olajuwon was joined by his former University of Houston teammate, Clyde "the Glide"

Drexler. Together, they helped Houston through a difficult postseason. To win their second straight championship, the Rockets had to defeat four excellent teams, all of which had **homecourt advantage**: the Utah Jazz, the Phoenix Suns, the San Antonio Spurs, and the Orlando Magic.

With a supporting cast that included Robert Horry, Sam Cassell, and Kenny Smith, the Rockets prevailed. Houston faced elimination games five times, winning all five. Only the finals—in which Olajuwon outclassed budding star Shaquille O'Neal of the Magic— were a breather. Houston swept Orlando in four games.

Olajuwon, who left Houston for the Toronto Raptors after the 2000–01 season, compiled career numbers that place him among the best players in league history. He is in the all-time top 10 in scoring and 11th in rebounding. He is the only center in the top 10 in steals and is the NBA's all-time blocked shots leader.

In 2002, the Rockets once again drafted a foreign-born center. Yao Ming, from China, is 7-foot-5. Yao not only has tremendous basketball skills, but also a winning personality, just like Olajuwon.

In his first NBA season, Yao averaged 13.5 points and 8.2 rebounds per game. He improved to 17.5 points and 9.0 rebounds the next year, and, along with guard Steve Francis, gave the Rockets an inside-outside combination that helped the team win 45 regular-season games in 2003–04 and advance to the playoffs for the first time in five seasons. Francis was gone the next season, but high-scoring guard Tracy McGrady complemented Yao, and Houston went 51–31 and made the postseason again.

Yao has not been able to deliver a postseason series win yet—a

Yao Ming hopes to propel the Rockets to another championship.

Houston coach Jeff Van Gundy is the brother of Miami Heat coach Stan Van Gundy.

tough, seven-game loss to Dallas kept Houston from advancing in 2004–05—but time will tell if the Rockets have another Dream on their hands. If they do, it will be a recurring nightmare for the rest of the NBA.

CHAPTER THREE

THE MEMPHIS GRIZZLIES

I n 1995, the Vancouver Grizzlies and the Toronto Raptors became the first NBA franchises to be based outside of the United States since 1947, when the Toronto Huskies folded. The Grizzlies finished in last place in the Midwest Division in their debut season. Their 15–67 record was the league's worst.

The season actually began well. Vancouver won its inaugural game, 92–80, at Portland. They followed that victory at home with a 100–98 defeat of the Minnesota Timberwolves.

Then reality hit. Vancouver lost 19 straight games, including a 49-point loss at San Antonio. Coach Brian Winters depended on a few savvy veterans, such as guards Greg Anthony (the team's leading scorer at 14.0 points per game) and Byron Scott, as well as 7-foot rookie center Bryant "Big Country" Reeves. The Grizzlies simply had a shortage of talent, and they later lost 23 consecutive games that first season.

Selecting third in the 1996 NBA draft, Vancouver chose 6-foot-9 forward Shareef Abdur-Rahim. The former University of California star had left Berkeley after becoming the first freshman in Pac-10 history to be named the conference's player of the year. He immediately became Vancouver's go-to player. He averaged 18.7 points per game in 1996–97, tops on the

Bryant Reeves, the first pick in Grizzlies' history, holds the franchise single-game scoring record. During the 1997–98 season, he exploded for 41 points against the Boston Celtics.

The 2002–03 Grizzlies featured five former All-Rookie first team members: Shane Battier, Pau Gasol, Brevin Knight, Mike Miller, and Jason Williams.

club. Instead of improving, though, Vancouver sank to 14–68 and again had the poorest record in the NBA.

In those early seasons, Vancouver's year-end win-loss records resembled dates on a history quiz: 15–67, 14–68, 19–63, and, in the strike-shortened 1999 season, 8–42. Abdur-Rahim did his best on poor teams. In 1998, his 22.3 points per game ranked sixth in the league.

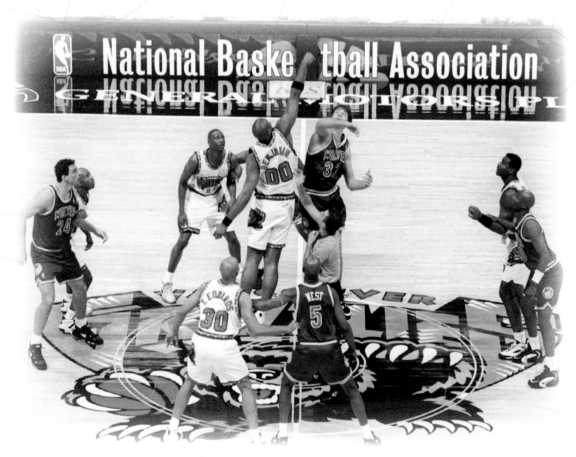

The Grizzlies (in the white uniforms), then in Vancouver, tipped it off at home for the first time against Minnesota in 1995.

Shareef Abdur-Rahim slams home two points for the Grizzlies.

Vancouver, in the province of British Columbia, is about three hours north of Seattle by car. Fans initially supported the team. Still, many players considered it to be the NBA's farthest **outpost.**

Talented Mike Bibby was an instant star at point guard.

In 1998, the Grizzlies used the second pick in the draft to take Mike Bibby, a gifted point guard. In 1999, they chose shooting guard Steve Francis from the University of Maryland. Francis immediately declared that he would never play for Vancouver, which left the franchise in a tight spot. They traded Francis (who would go on to share the NBA Rookie of the Year award) to Houston and received Bibby's former University of Arizona teammate Michael Dickerson, three other players, and a future draft pick in return.

That season, 1999–2000, Vancouver finished last in the Midwest (22–60) for the fourth time in its five years of existence. After the 2000–01 season, Bibby headed south to play for the Sacramento Kings. With attendance heading in the same direction, Vancouver decided to move the entire franchise south—to Memphis.

Hubie Brown, who retired from coaching 12 games into the 2004–05 season, was inducted into the Basketball Hall of Fame that year.

**Shane Battier (No. 31) and Pau Gasol (No. 16) team up to
make things difficult for Grizzlies' opponents.**

Abdur-Rahim, the nearest thing to a star that the franchise had, was
traded to the Atlanta Hawks.

The Memphis Grizzlies were almost an entirely new team, in
an entirely new location. New general manager Jerry West shrewdly
acquired a high draft pick for Abdur-Rahim, so that on draft day of 2001,

Memphis had two of the first six picks. They drafted 6-foot-10 forward Shane Battier, the national college player of the year, from Duke University. The Grizzlies also acquired Pau Gasol from Spain. Gasol had been drafted by Atlanta and then traded to the Grizzlies.

Both Gasol and Battier were named to the All-Rookie first team. Gasol averaged 17.6 points and 8.9 rebounds per game and was the 2002 Rookie of the Year.

Slowly but surely, the Grizzlies have improved. In 2002–03, West traded for 2001 Rookie of the Year Mike Miller. Aided by the talents of point guard Jason Williams and center Stromile Swift, the 2003 Grizzlies won 28 games.

That set the stage for the best season in club history in 2003–04. With a solid core of returning players familiar with each other, Memphis won 50 games and made the playoffs for the first time in its brief history. The Grizzlies were just 17–18 in early January before reeling off a club-record eight consecutive victories to establish themselves as a postseason contender.

Gasol led the team in several categories, including scoring (17.7 points per game); Miller and James Posey provided potent outside shooting; and Battier was a force on both offense and defense. West was named the league's executive of the year, and Hubie Brown was named the coach of the year.

That season, as well as 2004–05, ended with lopsided playoff defeats in the opening round. But clearly, the Grizzlies were headed in the right direction. It all began by migrating south and adding West.

Forward/center Strohmile Swift, who signed with Houston following the 2004–05 season, was the last remaining Grizzlies' player to have been with the club in Vancouver.

THE NEW ORLEANS HORNETS

The Hornets began playing in a state best known for its college basketball tradition and moved to a city famous for jazz music. Wherever they've played, they have brought youthful excitement and won over many new fans.

The NBA thought Charlotte would be a great place to put an **expansion team** in 1988. North Carolina was known for its passionate basketball fans, who followed hometown college teams such as Duke and Wake Forest. Many of those same fans filled the Charlotte Arena, known as the Hive, to see NBA play. The Hornets fed off that enthusiasm for 13 seasons in the Tar Heel state.

A number of those early Hornets became fan favorites. Point guard Tyrone "Muggsy" Bogues was only 5-foot-3, but he played with tremendous energy and competitive fire. Larry Johnson was drafted out of the University of Nevada–Las Vegas in 1991. "L J" became the team's leader and Muggsy's best friend. In 1992, the team added Georgetown University center Alonzo Mourning to its roster. Now the squad was complete. With Mourning's defense and rebounding setting the tone, the club made the playoffs in 1993. There they shocked the Boston Celtics, beating them in four games. The home fans went wild as Mourning's buzzer-beater sealed the victory for the Hornets.

Rap star Master P tried out with the Hornets in 1999.

Alonzo Mourning soars above the Heat for a slam dunk!

Glen Rice averaged 26.8 points for the Hornets' team that won 54 games in 1996–97.

The young team continued to grow. The Hornets made the playoffs again in 1995. In 1996, they said goodbye to Johnson and Mourning in a pair of trades that shocked and angered many fans. The team managed to win back the crowds the following season, however. New Hornets Glen Rice and Vlade Divac led the team to a franchise-record 54 victories. The Hive was buzzing again.

There were more changes to come. The team traded Bogues to Golden State in 1997. Players were saddened by the death of guard Bobby Phills in a car accident in 2000. But the biggest change of all came in 2002, when the team announced it would be moving to New Orleans for the 2002–03 season.

The former home of the New Orleans Jazz welcomed its new team with open arms. The Hornets did not disappoint, winning 47 games and remaining in the chase for the top conference seed in the playoffs until late in the season. Only a six-game loss to the Philadelphia 76ers in the opening round of the postseason put a damper on the year.

Muggsy Bogues is the shortest player in NBA history.

Guard Baron Davis played on Hornets' teams that reached the playoffs five consecutive seasons from 1999–2000 through 2003–04.

Guard David Wesley reached the 10,000-point mark for his career in 2004. He joined John Starks and Moses Malone as the only players to reach that plateau despite not being drafted.

Star forward Jamal Mashburn was hurt much of the following season, but guard Baron Davis and center Jamaal Magloire stepped up their games and earned All-Star berths. The Hornets made the playoffs for the seventh time in eight seasons despite finishing just 41–41.

Unfortunately, that turned out to be an indication of decline. Mashburn was traded to Philadelphia in the middle of the 2004–05 season, and the Hornets

High-scoring Jamal Mashburn averaged more than 20 points per game in each of his four full seasons with the Hornets.

The Hornets began rebuilding with players such as 2005 draft picks Chris Paul (No. 3) and Brandon Bass (No. 1).

The Hornets selected Wake Forest point guard Chris Paul with the fourth overall choice in the 2005 draft.

went into full rebuilding mode when Davis was shipped to Golden State at the trade deadline later in the year. New Orleans slumped to just 18 wins and finished in last place in the Southwest Division's first year.

CHAPTER FIVE

THE SAN ANTONIO SPURS

I n recent seasons, the Spurs have become the dominant team in the NBA. They won the league title in 2004–05 for the third time in seven seasons.

Winning is nothing new for San Antonio, however. Since joining the NBA prior to the 1976–77 season, the Spurs have consistently been a winner. Only three times in their NBA history have the Spurs failed to win at least 30 games.

The Spurs were born in 1967, in a different Texas town in a different league. A charter member of the American Basketball Association (ABA), the Spurs began as the Dallas Chaparrals. The franchise moved to San Antonio in 1973 and was renamed the Spurs.

In 1976, San Antonio became one of four teams from the ABA to join the NBA and was placed in the Central Division. The team's big star was silky smooth 6-foot-8 shooter George Gervin. "The Iceman," as he was known, was an incredible scoring machine.

With his patented **finger-roll** and deadly jumper, the Iceman led the league in scoring in four different

"The Admiral" just barely won the league scoring title in 1993–94. With George Gervin watching in the stands, David Robinson scored 71 points in the final game of the season to edge Shaquille O'Neal of the Orlando Magic, 29.8 points per game to 29.3. Robinson's 71 points is the seventh-highest output in NBA history. Gervin's and Robinson's scoring titles were the two most closely contested in NBA history.

seasons (only Wilt Chamberlain and Michael Jordan have claimed more scoring titles). He once scored 63 points on the final day of one season to win a scoring title by less than .10 point per game. His most prolific scoring season was 1979–80, when he averaged 33.1 points per game.

Gervin helped the Spurs to the playoffs in 1979, but the result was heartbreaking. The Spurs led the Eastern Conference Finals three games to one but then lost three straight. The final loss, a 107–105 pulse-racer, ended when Washington's Elvin Hayes blocked a shot by Spurs guard James Silas at the buzzer.

"The Iceman," George Gervin, won four NBA scoring titles.

In 1995, center David Robinson became the first San Antonio player to be named the league's MVP.

That was as close as Spurs' fans came to seeing a championship for a long time. San Antonio moved to the Midwest Division in the Western Conference in 1980. The team won three consecutive division titles. Gervin's scoring, however, paled against the many weapons of the Los Angeles Lakers, who routed San Antonio in the Western Conference finals in both 1982 and 1983.

In 1987, San Antonio, picking first in the NBA draft for the very first time, selected 7-foot center David Robinson from the United States Naval Academy. But

On March 6, 1982, San Antonio defeated the Milwaukee Bucks 171–166 in triple overtime. It is the second-highest scoring game in NBA history. George Gervin scored 24 of his 50 points in overtime and knocked down the final seven shots that he attempted.

Sean Elliott (left) was skilled on both offense and defense.

the Spurs had to wait for "the Admiral" to fulfill a two-year military commitment before he could join the league.

In 1989, Robinson started play, along with forward Sean Elliott. Two of the league's best community leaders off the court, as well as All-Stars on it, Robinson and Elliott reversed the franchise's course. San Antonio went from 21 wins the previous season to 56 the next. The 35-victory leap was an NBA record. The Admiral—averaging 24.3 points, 12.0 rebounds, and 3.89 blocked shots per game—was a shoo-in for Rookie of the Year.

In 1994–95, Robinson steered the franchise to uncharted waters. For the first time, San Antonio finished with the league's best record,

62–20. Robinson became the Spurs' first league MVP, averaging 27.6 points per contest.

Before the 1998–99 season, the Spurs chose 7-footer Tim Duncan, a native of the U.S. Virgin Islands. Blessed with a graceful bank shot and a calm manner, Duncan teamed with Robinson and Elliott to give San Antonio an excellent **frontcourt.** It was perhaps the NBA's best since the Boston Celtics' trio of Hall of Famers (Larry Bird, Kevin McHale, and Robert Parish) a decade earlier.

Duncan followed in the Admiral's footsteps, winning the Rookie of the Year award in 1998 and MVP in 2002 and 2003. In 1998–99, Duncan was among the league leaders in scoring and rebounding as San Antonio won its first NBA championship.

The Spurs were magnificent that postseason. San Antonio, which shared the league's top regular-season record (37–13) with the Utah Jazz, swept two series and finished 15–2 overall in the playoffs. In the NBA Finals, the Spurs defeated the New York Knicks, 4–1.

In 2002–03, Robinson's last season, San Antonio won its second title. On the way, the Spurs defeated the three-time defending champion Lakers. In the finals, they downed the New Jersey Nets, four games to two.

With the Admiral retired, the franchise's fortunes fell squarely on Duncan's shoulders, and the big man has proved to be more than capable. The Spurs narrowly missed winning the Midwest Division championship in 2003–04 and swept Memphis in the opening round of the playoffs before the Lakers stopped them.

While playing for the Spurs, guard Alvin Robertson twice led the league in steals (1986 and 1987), and forward George Johnson twice led the NBA in blocked shots (1981 and 1982).

That proved to be only a brief setback, however. In 2004–05, San Antonio went 59–23 during the regular season and edged Dallas by a single game to win the first Southwest Division crown. Duncan averaged 20.3 points and 11.1 rebounds during the regular season, and got considerable help from guards Tony Parker, a native of France, and acrobatic Manu Ginobili, an import from Argentina.

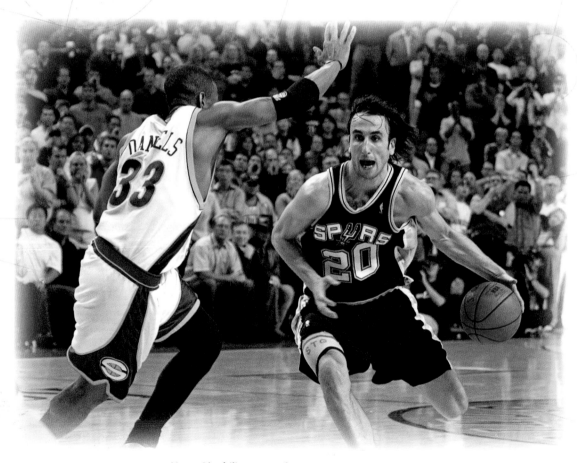

Manu Ginobili averaged 16.0 points per game for the Spurs' league champions in 2004–05.

Center Tim Duncan has helped keep the Spurs among the NBA's elite teams.

In the playoffs, San Antonio had little trouble dispatching Denver, Seattle, and Phoenix to reach the NBA Finals. There, the Spurs battled the defending-champion Pistons in a classic seven-game series. Duncan scored 25 points and pulled down 11 boards in the decisive Game 7, a hard-fought 81–74 triumph.

When they returned home, the Spurs enjoyed a victory parade by traveling on barges down the San Antonio River. Some 350,000 fans joined them in celebrating the club's third NBA crown since 1999.

Center Tim Duncan earned his third NBA Finals MVP award in 2005. The only others with three or more are superstars Michael Jordan (6), Magic Johnson (3), and Shaquille O'Neal (3).

TIME LINE

1967 The Rockets (then located in San Diego) and Spurs (then in the ABA and located in Dallas) are founded

1971 The Rockets move to Houston

1976 The San Antonio Spurs join the NBA

1980 The Dallas Mavericks join the NBA as an expansion team

1988 The Hornets begin play as an expansion team in Charlotte

1994 The Houston Rockets win the first of back-to-back NBA championships

1995 The Memphis Grizzlies are founded as the Vancouver Grizzlies

1999 San Antonio captures the NBA title

2001 The Grizzlies move to Memphis

2002 The Hornets move to New Orleans

2003 San Antonio wins its second NBA championship

2004 The Grizzlies post a winning record and make the playoffs for the first time

2005 The Spurs win the NBA title for the second time in three years and the third time over all

STAT STUFF

TEAM RECORDS

TEAM	ALL-TIME RECORD	NBA TITLES (MOST RECENT)	NUMBER OF TIMES IN PLAYOFFS	TOP COACH (WINS)
Dallas	924–1,094	0	11	Don Nelson (339)
Houston	1,543–1,541	2 (1994–95)	23	Rudy Tomjanovich (503)
Memphis	247–541	0	2	Hubie Brown (83)
New Orleans	648–714	0	9	Paul Silas (208)
San Antonio	*1,750–1,340	3 (2004–05)	*33	Gregg Popovich (455)

*includes ABA

NBA SOUTHWEST CAREER LEADERS (THROUGH 2004–05)

TEAM	CATEGORY	NAME (YEARS WITH TEAM)	TOTAL
Dallas	Points	Rolando Blackman (1981–92)	16,643
	Rebounds	James Donaldson (1985–92)	4,589
Houston	Points	Hakeem Olajuwon (1984–2001)	26,511
	Rebounds	Hakeem Olajuwon (1984–2001)	13,382
Memphis	Points	Shareef Abdur-Rahim (1996–2001)	7,801
	Rebounds	Shareef Abdur-Rahim (1996–2001)	3,070
New Orleans	Points	Dell Curry (1988–98)	9,839
	Rebounds	Larry Johnson (1991–95)	3,479
San Antonio	Points	David Robinson (1989–2003)	20,790
	Rebounds	David Robinson (1989–2003)	10,497

MORE STAT STUFF

MEMBERS OF THE NAISMITH MEMORIAL NATIONAL
BASKETBALL HALL OF FAME

DALLAS PLAYER	POSITION	DATE INDUCTED
Alex English	Forward	1997

NEW ORLEANS PLAYER	POSITION	DATE INDUCTED
Robert Parish	Center	2003

HOUSTON PLAYER	POSITION	DATE INDUCTED
Rick Barry	Guard	1987
Clyde Drexler	Guard	2004
Alex Hannum	Coach	1998
Elvin Hayes	Forward/Center	1990
Moses Malone	Forward/Center	2001
Calvin Murphy	Guard	1993

SAN ANTONIO PLAYER	POSITION	DATE INDUCTED
George Gervin	Forward	1996
Moses Malone	Center	2001

MEMPHIS PLAYER	POSITION	DATE INDUCTED
Hubie Brown	Contributor	2005

Moses Malone played for both the Houston Rockets and the San Antonio Spurs during a pro career that spanned 21 seasons.

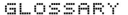

GLOSSARY

buzzer-beater—a shot that wins a game just as the game-ending buzzer sounds

disbanded—broke up; ceased to exist

draft—an annual selection of college players by a pro sports league

expansion team—in sports, this means a team created from scratch and added to a league

finger-roll—a type of shot made close to the basket in which the player reaches high over his head and rolls the ball off his fingertips into the basket

goaltend—to block a shot as it is coming down toward the basket; this is an illegal play and the referees will award the basket and the points to the shooting team

homecourt advantage—what a team has when it will play more games in a playoff series at its home arena; most teams have greater success playing in front of their home fans

low post—the area beneath and around the basket, where taller players do most of their work

NBA Finals—a seven-game series between the winners of the NBA's Eastern and Western Conference championships

outpost—an outlying branch of an organization, in this case the NBA

power forward—a tall, strong player who is depended upon for scoring and rebounding

sixth man—a basketball team's key substitute, the first player off the bench after the starting five

FOR MORE INFORMATION ABOUT
THE SOUTHWEST DIVISION AND THE NBA

BOOKS

Bradley, Michael. *Yao Ming.* New York: Benchmark Books, 2005.

Frisch, Aaron. *The History of the Dallas Mavericks.* Mankato, Minn.: Creative Education, 2002.

Frisch, Aaron. *The History of the Houston Rockets.* Mankato, Minn.: Creative Education, 2002.

Frisch, Aaron. *The History of the San Antonio Spurs.* Mankato, Minn.: Creative Education, 2002.

Gentile, Derek. *Smooth Moves: Juking, Jamming, Hooking & Slamming: Basketball's Players, Action & Style.* New York: Black Dog & Leventhal Publishers, 2003.

Goodman, Michael E. *The History of the Memphis Grizzlies.* Mankato, Minn.: Creative Education, 2002.

Hareas, John. *Basketball.* New York: DK Publishers, 2005.

Hudson, David L. *Basketball's Most Wanted II: The Top 10 Book of More Hotshot Hoopsters, Double Dribbles, and Roundball Oddities.* Washington, D.C.: Potomac Books, Inc., 2005.

Owens, Tom. *Basketball Arenas.* Brookfield, Conn.: Millbrook Press, 2002.

Savage, Jeff. *Yao Ming.* Minneapolis: LernerSports, 2005.

ON THE WEB

Visit our home page for lots of links
about The Southwest Division teams:
http://www.childsworld.com/links

Note to Parents, Teachers, and Librarians: We routinely verify our Web links to make
sure they are safe, active sites—so encourage your readers to check them out!

INDEX

ABOUT THE AUTHORS

John Walters is a former staff writer at *Sports Illustrated* who worked at the magazine from 1989 to 2001. He is the author of two other books: *Basketball for Dummies,* which he co-wrote with former Notre Dame basketball coach Digger Phelps; and *The Same River Twice: A Season with Geno Auriemma and the Connecticut Huskies,* which chronicles the women's basketball team's 2000–01 season.

Robert E. Schnakenberg has written eight books on sports for young readers, including *Teammates: John Stockton and Karl Malone* and *Scottie Pippen: Reluctant Superstar.* He lives in Brooklyn, New York.